THE KING of IRELAND'S SON

Brendan Behan

Illustrated by P. J. Lynch

Orchard Books

New York

Once upon a time, and a very good time it was too, when the streets were paved with penny loaves and houses were whitewashed with buttermilk and the pigs ran round with knives and forks in their snouts shouting, "Eat me, eat me!" there lived a King of Ireland and he had three sons named Art, Neart and Ceart. Art is a man's name simply, Neart means "strength" and Ceart means "right" or "justice." At one particular time, you could hear, all around the country, heavenly music coming from somewhere, and the King wanted to know where it was coming from. So he said to his three sons, "Go out and whichever of you finds out where the heavenly music is coming from can have half my kingdom."

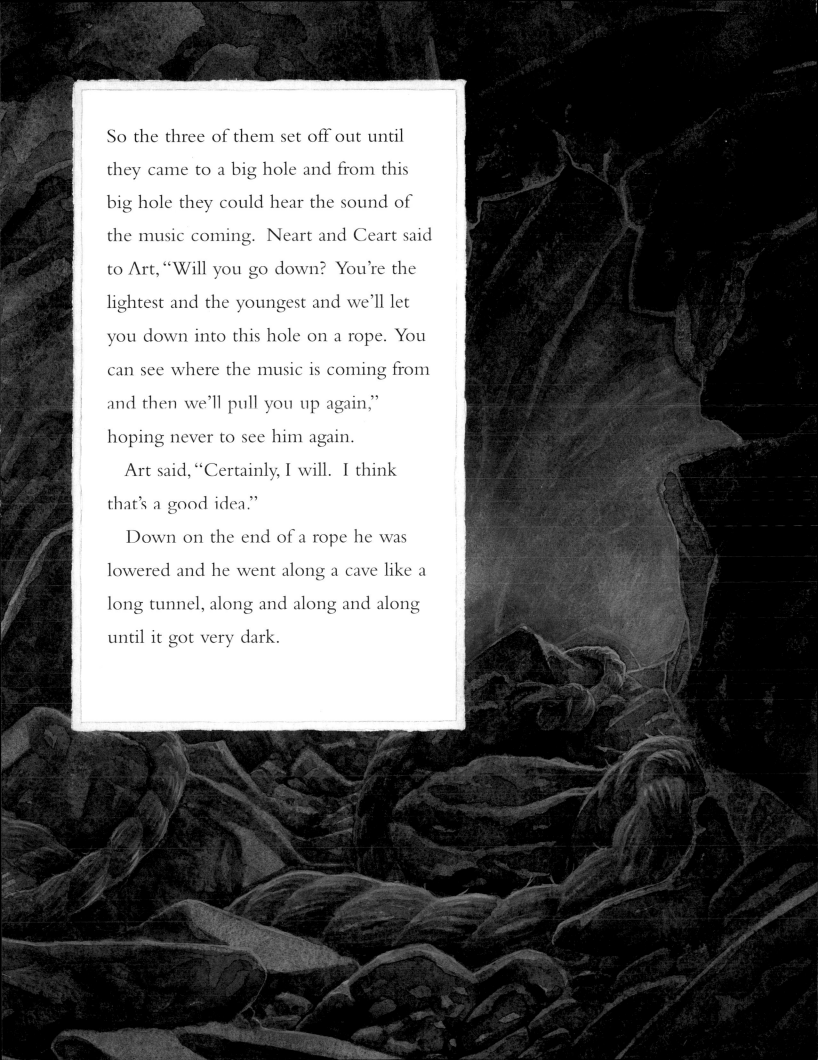

So the three of them set off out until they came to a big hole and from this big hole they could hear the sound of the music coming. Neart and Ceart said to Art, "Will you go down? You're the lightest and the youngest and we'll let you down into this hole on a rope. You can see where the music is coming from and then we'll pull you up again," hoping never to see him again.

Art said, "Certainly, I will. I think that's a good idea."

Down on the end of a rope he was lowered and he went along a cave like a long tunnel, along and along and along until it got very dark.

"No, then," said the man, "I can't. But I tell you what you can do. You can stop the night and tomorrow you can walk—it's a day's journey—on to my father's place and he might be able to tell you."

So the old man put him up for the night and gave him the best of food. They had rashers and eggs with black pudding and white pudding and a Cork drisheen, three Hafner's sausages each, the best of homemade wholemeal bread, all washed down with lashings of strong tea, and after that they both went to bed, as well they might after such a feed.

He walked for hours until it must have been night-time, for in the tunnel he couldn't tell night from day. In the end and when his feet were falling off him, he saw a light. Over to the light he went and he met an old man and he said to the old man that was there, "Could you tell me where the heavenly music is coming from?"

The next morning Art woke up and started on his journey for another day's travelling along the tunnel, until he came to another light and he went in and met an old, old man and he said to him, "Are you the father of the other old man that I saw back along there?"

"That's not an old man," said the second old man. "He's only a hundred."

"Well," said Art, "I'd like to know where the heavenly music is coming from and he said you might be able to help me."

"Well," said the second old man, "that I can't help you. But my father that lives further up might be able to. Come in anyway and I'll feed you for the night and you can get up in the morning and go up and ask my father."

So Art went in and the old, old man gave him a great meal. They had

bowls of stirabout, followed by huge plates of best Limerick ham with spring cabbage and lovely potatoes that were like balls of flour melting in your mouth, and with all this they drank three pints each of the freshest buttermilk Art had ever tasted. I can tell you that he slept soundly that night.

And the next morning he got up and after saying goodbye to the old, old man, he walked for another whole day along the tunnel until he came to another light and there was an old, old, old man. So Art said to him, "Are you the father of the old, old man back there along the tunnel?"

"Well, I am," said the old, old, old man, "but that fellow's not as old as he makes out; he's only a hundred and fifty and he eats all them new-fangled foods, as you probably found out."

"Well," said Art, "he did me very well. But what I wanted to know was if you can tell me where the heavenly music comes from?"

"Well, now," said the old, old, old man, "we'll talk about that in the morning. Come on in now and have a bit to eat and rest yourself. You must be famished after that day's walking."

So in Art went and the old, old, old man got some food ready. They started off with two great bowls of yellow buck porridge each and after that they had four crubeens apiece with fresh soda bread and homemade butter and they had three pints of the creamiest porter Art had ever drunk to go with it all.

The next morning, he got up and he said to the old man, "Now can you tell me where the heavenly music is coming from?"

"Well, no," said the old, old, old man, "but I know there's nobody else living at the end of this tunnel except a terrible fierce man, a giant, and," he said, "I wouldn't go near him if I were you. But if you do decide to go up to him, he lives a terrible far distance away at the very end. You'll find, however," he said, "a little stallion when you go a couple of miles up the road there and, if you get up on him, he'll carry you to where the heavenly music comes from. But," he said, "you'll want to be very wary of that giant."

Art went along and he came up to where, sure enough, there was a stallion and there was light with more light further on. So the stallion said to him, "Do you want a lift?"

"I do," said Art, "but I'm going up to where the heavenly music is."

"Well, that's all right," said the stallion, "no offence given and no offence taken. Jump up there on my back and I'll take you."

So up on the stallion's back he jumped and galloped away for nearly a whole day, until he came to one of the most beautiful gardens Art had ever seen. "This," said the stallion, "is the nearest I can take you to where the heavenly music comes from."

Art went up through the garden, wondering at every more marvellous thing that he saw. Nearer and nearer came the heavenly music and at last Art came to a house and the music was coming from there. Into the house Art went and there was the most beautiful girl he had ever seen. And she was singing and making heavenly music.

"Good morning," said Art, and then he said quickly, "Don't let me interrupt your song, which is the loveliest I've ever heard."

"Oh!" she answered him. "I'm glad you've interrupted it. I have to make music here for an old giant that captured me. I'm the King of Greece's daughter," she said, "and I've been here for a year and a day and I can't get away from this old fellow until someone comes to rescue me.

13

But," she said, "I'd sooner you went away, for he's a very big man and very, very fierce."

"I'm not afraid of him," said Art. "What can he do?"

"Well," she said, "he'll ask you a number of riddles. He has to hide for three nights and you have to hide for three nights—"

Before she could finish, or before Art could say whether he was going to stay or go, he heard a deep voice saying, "Who is this I see in here?" In comes this huge giant and caught poor Art by the throat. "What are you doing here?" he roared.

"I came to find the heavenly music," said Art.

"Well, now you've found it," said the giant, "and much good may it do you. And I'll tell you something," he said. "I'm going to hide for three days and, if you don't find me before the three days are up, I'll cut your head off, skin you, cook you and eat you.

"And after that," he roared, "if you have found me, you'll hide for three days and if I find you, I'll kill, skin, cook and eat you."

So poor Art didn't know what to say but, "Well, I'd like to go back and see to my little stallion."

"Right," said the giant, "but we'll start in the morning."

"This is an awful thing," said Art to the stallion when he got back. "What am I going to do—how do I know where he's going to hide?"

"That's all right," said the stallion. "It's getting late at night so we'll want to eat something, for, honest to God, my belly thinks my throat is cut. Sit down there now," said the stallion, "and put your left hand into my right ear and you'll find a tablecloth. Spread out the tablecloth," he said, and Art did as he was told. "Now," said the stallion, "put your right hand into my left ear and take out what you'll find there." Art did that and took out the best of fine food and the finest of old drink. "Now," said the stallion,

"you take that for yourself and stick your right hand into my left ear again." So Art did that and pulled out a bucket of water and a truss of hay. And Art ate the best of fine food and the finest of old drink and the stallion had the hay and the water. "Now," said the stallion when they were finished, "spread yourself out under my legs and we'll go to sleep for the night." So they went to sleep for the night.

The next morning when they woke up, they could hear the giant shouting, "Now come and find me if you can."

"I can tell you where he is," the little stallion said to Art. "He's at the top of the tree."

So Art climbed to the top of the tree and there, right enough, was the giant who comes down very highly annoyed. "Aah!" he roared. "You found me today, but you won't find me tomorrow."

After this, Art had great confidence in the stallion; and that night, he
again had a feed of the best of fine food and the finest of old drink,
and the stallion had a truss of hay and a bucket of clear water, and
they carried on a learned discussion until it was time to go to bed.

Next morning when they got up, the stallion said, "Now
go on in through the house and out into the
back garden and there you'll see a football.
Give the football a good kick."

"All right," said Art, and off he
went and, in the back garden, he
gave the football a terrific kick and
out spun the giant.

"Well," said the giant very nastily, "you got me this time, but you won't get me tomorrow, for I've got a trick up my sleeve yet."

Art went back to the stallion and told him what had happened and said, "What will we do now?"

"Well," said the stallion, "first of all, we'll have a feed." They ate again, all kinds of lovely foods, and talked until it was time to go to sleep.

In the morning, Art said, "What will I do now? Where is he hiding?"

"I'll tell you what to do," said the stallion. "When you go inside, ask the girl where he is. But," he said, "without the giant understanding you. Just signal to her, where is he?"

So Art goes and sees the daughter of the King of Greece and she is singing away there and he makes signs to ask where is the giant. The girl pointed to a ring on her finger and, at first, Art didn't understand. But she motioned him to take the ring off, which he did. He looked at it and made signs to show that he didn't believe that the giant could fit in such a small ring. But the girl kept singing away and pointed him to throw it in the fire. So he did that and there was an enormous screech, "Oh! I'm burnt! I'm burnt!" and out jumped the giant. "Now," he roared, "you caught me the three times, but now it's your turn."

"All right," said Art, "I'll hide tomorrow."

"Well, now," said Art to the stallion when he went back, "we're in a right fix now. Where am I going to hide? Sure I'm a stranger here and don't know the place."

"That's all right," said the stallion. "I'll tell you in the morning. In the meantime, put your hands into my two ears and take out the grub." So they had a feed and then Art got under the stallion's legs and slept there for the night.

When he woke up, "Now," said the stallion, "the first thing you do is to take a hair out of my tail, and the hole it leaves, get up into that." So Art took the hair out of the stallion's tail, got up into the hole and stopped there. And the giant searched all round and couldn't find Art all day and nearly went tearing mad. Art came out that night and the giant said, "I didn't find you today, but I'll find you tomorrow and eat you."

So that night Art said to the stallion, "Where am I going to hide tomorrow?"

"That's all right," said the stallion. "Put your hands into my two ears and take out the food and we'll have a feed first. Then you can stretch out under my legs and have a sleep and we'll talk about the matter in the morning."

In the morning Art said, "Now where am I going to hide?"

"Take a nail out of my hoof," said the stallion, "get up into the hole and draw the nail up after you." So Art did that and stayed there all day, while the giant went round roaring and swearing.

At night, the giant went back to his house and Art came out of the hole and said, "So you didn't find me."

"No," said the giant, "but I will tomorrow and then I'll skin, cook and eat you."

Then Art said to the stallion, "Where will I hide tomorrow?" and the stallion said, "One thing at a time. Get out the grub there and we'll have a good feed and we'll see about the other matter in the morning."

"Now," said the stallion in the morning, when they woke up fresh and early, "pull out one of my teeth, get up into the hole and draw the tooth up after you." The giant came rampaging around the place and couldn't find Art and, to cut a long story short, he nearly went demented.

In the evening, Art came out and went into the house and there was the King of Greece's daughter. The music was stopped, but she looked happier than ever and she said, "You have broken the spell. I had to wait for a stranger to come and beat the giant six times."

"We've done that," said Art. "Now I'll take you away from here."

"All right," she said, "although I'm the daughter of the King of Greece."

"Well," said Art, "that's nothing. I'm the King of Ireland's son." So she jumped up on the back of the stallion behind Art and they rode out of the tunnel back to his father's palace.

The King of Greece's daughter then sang some of the heavenly music for the King of Ireland and the King gave Art half his kingdom. The two brothers were banished and Art and the King of Greece's daughter got married and

they had a wedding and everybody ate and drank, and wasn't I at the wedding as well as everybody else and I got a present of a pair of paper boots and a pair of stockings make of buttermilk; and that's the end of my story and all I'm going to tell you.

For Luke

Text copyright © 1962 by Brendan Behan from *Brendan Behan's Island — An Irish Sketchbook* by Brendan Behan and Paul Hogarth (Hutchinson, 1962). Illustrations copyright © 1996 by P. J. Lynch.

Orchard Books
95 Madison Avenue
New York, NY 10016

Color separated in Italy by Fotoriproduzioni Grafiche
Printed and bound in Italy by Grafiche AZ, Verona

10 9 8 7 6 5 4 3 2 1

Library of Congress Cataloging-in-Publication Data
Behan, Brendan.
The King of Ireland's son/Brendan Behan ; illustrated by P.J. Lynch. -- 1st American ed.
p. cm.
"First published in Great Britain in 1996 by Andersen Press, Ltd."--Copyr. p.
Summary: Sent to find the source of the heavenly music heard throughout the kingdom,
the youngest son of the King of Ireland finds a beautiful maiden held captive by a fierce giant.
ISBN 0-531-09549-5
[1. Fairy tales. 2. Folklore--Ireland.] I. Lynch, Patrick James, ill. II. Title.
PZ8.B393Ki 1997 398.2--dc20 [E] 96-28377